CIRIA C636

Investing in tomorrow's company
Improving sustainability communications between property and construction companies and the investment community

J Hirigoyen   Upstream
G Chant-Hall CIRIA
S Reid   CIRIA

CIRIA *sharing knowledge ■ building best practice*

Classic House, 174–180 Old Street, London EC1V 9BP, UK
TEL +44 (0)20 7549 3300   FAX +44 (0)20 7253 0523
EMAIL enquiries@ciria.org
WEBSITE www.ciria.org

Summary

Environmental and social performance is of increasing importance to both SRI and mainstream/traditional investors, as they realise that these issues can influence economic performance and commercial risk. This trend to wider reporting of risks and their economic impacts is mirrored in tightening regulation such as the Turnbull Guidance and the Draft Regulations on the Operating and Financial Review.

It is in the best interest of both property (real estate) and construction companies, and the investment community they address, to reach a common understanding of the most relevant social, ethical, economic and environmental (or sustainability) risks and opportunities faced by companies in these sectors. Such risks and opportunities can differ significantly according to the company's activities across these industry sectors. It is up to companies to identify and prioritise and effectively manage the most relevant issues that could impact on their financial performance, using a systematic, comprehensive and transparent process.

This guide provides a walk through of the key steps of such a process for companies in the property and construction sectors, including guidance on how to:

- understand how investors might make decisions and how providing sustainability information might influence this process
- identify and prioritise the key sustainability issues that are most relevant to their business, considering:
  - the stage of the property development, construction and investment process in which they are involved
  - the company's key characteristics and external context (policy issues and stakeholder concerns)
- link sustainability performance with financial performance in all communications with investors
- measure, monitor and manage the key sustainability issues effectively
- develop a sustainability communications strategy appropriate for investors, considering both non-financial reporting requirements and other communication media.

Understanding how sustainability issues might affect the performance of companies in the property and construction sectors should assist SRI and mainstream investors to make better informed investment decisions.

It is believed that if both companies and investors work to the principles explained in this guide, it will assist the evolution of an industry-wide conceptual framework for reporting.

Investing in tomorrow's company.
Hirigoyen, J; Chant-Hall, G; Reid, S
CIRIA
C636   © CIRIA 2005   RP696   ISBN 0-86017-636-3

Keywords
Benchmarking and KPIs, environmental good practice, respect for people, social responsibility, sustainable construction.

Reader interest	Classification	
(Listed) real estate and construction companies: executive and non-executive directors, sustainability/CSR managers, investor relations and corporate communications officers. Investment community: buy and sell side analysts, fund managers, pension fund trustees, financial analysts, corporate financiers/investment bankers.	AVAILABILITY	Unrestricted
	CONTENT	Advice/guidance
	STATUS	Committee-guided
	USER	Property and construction companies, SRI and mainstream investment analysts

Published by CIRIA, Classic House, 174–180 Old Street, London EC1V 9BP, UK.

British Library Cataloguing in Publication Data
A catalogue record is available for this book from the British Library.

All rights reserved. No part of this publication may be reproduced or transmitted in any form or by any means, including photocopying and recording, without the written permission of the copyright-holder, application for which should be addressed to the publisher. Such written permission must also be obtained before any part of this publication is stored in a retrieval system of any nature.

This publication is designed to provide accurate and authoritative information in regard to the subject matter covered. It is sold and/or distributed with the understanding that neither the authors nor the publisher is thereby engaged in rendering a specific legal or any other professional service. While every effort has been made to ensure the accuracy and completeness of the publication, no warranty or fitness is provided or implied, and the authors and publisher shall have neither liability nor responsibility to any person or entity with respect to any loss or damage arising from its use.

Foreword

Improved corporate reporting is a key business issue today. Its importance is reflected in initiatives from government, such as the proposal to introduce a mandatory Operating and Financial Review for all quoted companies, but also in the increasing realisation on the part of investors that the value of their investment is, potentially, affected by a very wide range of factors, many of which have not been adequately reflected in conventional, financially based company reports. Investors recognise that decisions by all kinds of stakeholders – employees, customers, suppliers, society more widely – will affect long-term shareholder value, and companies in many sectors are, as a consequence, recognising that they need to communicate much more effectively about the ethical, social, economic and environmental risks and opportunities that they face. In this way improved reporting is not just a response to regulatory pressure from government but a tool to enhance business competitiveness.

Many companies also recognise that they have some way to go in improving their own understanding of these "sustainability" issues and deciding how best to report on them. That is why the publication of this Guide is particularly to be welcomed. It provides a clear and concise map for companies in the property (real estate) and construction sectors that will enable them to improve their understanding of investor perceptions, to identify the key risks and opportunities most relevant to their business, and to decide how best to report on performance. In my view the principles set out in the Guide have the potential to help companies significantly to improve not only their reporting but also their understanding of the factors driving performance in their own business.

As we look ahead to the introduction of the mandatory OFR, the focus of directors will increasingly need to be on how to ensure that their OFR meets the requirements of the Regulations, and in particular meets the OFR objective of providing the information that will enable members to assess the company's strategies and their potential to succeed. This Guide will give directors an excellent start in deciding how to exercise these responsibilities. But for those who follow where the guidance leads, it will also, potentially, be a trigger for improved business performance, and for competitive advantage in the market for investment funds.

Rosemary Radcliffe, January 2005

Rosemary Radcliffe CBE is an economist and business consultant. She served on the steering group for the Review of Company Law that recommended the introduction of a mandatory OFR and she chaired the independent working group set up by the DTI to develop practical guidance on the OFR for directors.

Acknowledgements

This report is a result of the CIRIA and Upstream research project RP696 "Investing in tomorrow's company", which was undertaken by an Upstream project team with input from CIRIA.

Lead author

Julie Hirigoyen is a director of Upstream. Julie has spent more than six years working with property developers and investors to establish and implement robust sustainability strategies, and to communicate these effectively to stakeholders. She has an in-depth knowledge of the property industry and a background in law and sustainable development.

Co-authors

Greg Chant-Hall is a project manager with CIRIA. He has an established track record in the environmental and construction sectors and has worked with many construction companies including clients, designers, and contractors of all sizes. Greg is a registered environmental auditor and a member of IEMA, CIWEM and CIWM.

Sarah Reid is a project manager with CIRIA, and has overseen a wide variety of projects, including the development of guidance for construction clients on social responsibility, off-site production, disabled access in buildings and the refurbishment of occupied buildings.

Project funders

The project was funded by:

- The British Land Company plc
- CIRIA members
- Crest Nicholson plc
- DTI Partners in Innovation scheme
- Heathrow Terminal 5: BAA plc and WSP group plc
- Land Securities Group plc
- Workspace Group plc.

CIRIA and Upstream would like to thank and acknowledge members of the project steering group for their significant contributions throughout the project. The steering group comprised:

Geoff Johnson (chair)	Land Securities Group plc
Andrew Armstrong	WSP Group plc
Claudine Blamey	The British Land Company plc
Kate Cairns	WSP Group plc
Caroline Cook	Business in the Community
Paul Donnelly	Crest Nicholson plc
Sarah Durham	Formerly of Jupiter Asset Management Ltd
Melissa Gamble	Morley Fund Management
Douglas Janikiewicz	Carillion plc
Beverley Lister	BAA plc
Lawrence Mbugua	Davis Langdon LLP (representing DTI)
Kirsty Sargent	F&C Asset Management plc (formerly ISIS Asset Management plc)
Mark Taylor	Workspace Group plc
Susie Wood	Jupiter Asset Management ltd

Contributions do not imply that individual funders, contributors or steering group members necessarily endorse all views expressed in this publication.

CIRIA's project managers were Greg Chant-Hall and Sarah Reid.

Many other organisations were consulted throughout the development of the guide by means of interviews and a consultation workshop.

Amec plc
Arup
Association of British Insurers
AWG plc
Balfour Beatty plc
Bovis Lend Lease Ltd
Construction Products Association
Countryside Properties plc
EIRIS Services Ltd
Hammerson plc
Henderson Global Investors Ltd
HSBC
Kingston University
MJ Gleeson Group plc
Slough Estates plc
The Berkeley Group plc
UK Social Investment Forum.

Contents

Summary 2
Foreword 3
Acknowledgements 4
Abbreviations and terms 6
Selected issues glossary 7

1 **Introduction** 9
   1.1 Why use this guide 9
   1.2 Who should use this guide 10
   1.3 How to use this guide 10

2 **What to communicate** 11
   2.1 Understanding how investors make decisions 11
   2.2 Defining the boundaries of "relevance" .. 11
   2.3 Demonstrating a systematic approach ... 15
   2.4 Hypothetical case studies 15

3 **How to communicate** 21
   3.1 Measuring, monitoring and managing ... 21
   3.2 Developing a sustainability communications strategy 22
   3.3 Non-financial reporting 23
   3.4 Communication media 24
   3.5 Assurance and verification 24

4 **Conclusions** 25

Appendices 26

A1 **Key facts** 26
A2 **Sources of further information** .. 28
   A2.1 Indicators, benchmarks and standards .. 28
   A2.2 Good practice guidance 30
   A2.3 Useful organisations 32

Figures

Fig 1 An example of how investors make decisions 12
Fig 2 Sustainability issues according to the stage of the development process 14
Fig 3 Example of a systematic approach 16
Fig 4 Hypothetical case studies: house-builders 18
Fig 5 Hypothetical case studies: construction contractors 19
Fig 6 Hypothetical case studies: commercial property companies 20

Tables

Table 1 Comparison between *Investing in tomorrow's company* and the OFR *Practical guidance for directors* 10
Table 2 Examples of links between sustainability and business success in the property and construction sectors 11
Table 3 Top tips when identifying the most relevant sustainability issues 13
Table 4 Measuring, monitoring and managing sustainability in property and construction activities 21
Table 5 Key considerations for communicating sustainability to investors 22
Table 6 Sustainability communications with investors 23

Abbreviations and terms

ABI The *Association of British Insurers* is the trade association for the UK's insurance industry, representing around 400 companies and nearly a quarter of all shares listed on the London Stock Exchange. The ABI has developed a series of guidelines including a guide on SRI.

AR&A *Annual report and accounts*. All publicly listed companies are required by law to produce an annual set of externally-audited accounts, with legal requirements for their content.

CSR The term *corporate social responsibility* is used (by companies) to describe the integration of social and environmental concerns in their business operations and their interaction with stakeholders.

DTI The *Department of Trade and Industry* is the UK government department that works to create a good environment for doing business in the UK by promoting enterprise, innovation and creativity. Website: <www.dti.gov.uk>.

NGO *Non-government organisations* are groups working to raise the profile of issues to corporations, governments and wider society. They often focus on specific issues, such as human rights or environmental impact, and can influence behaviour through their campaigning activities.

OFR *Operating and financial review*. See Appendix 2, item 36.

PFI The *Private Finance Initiative* is a means of funding major new public building projects such as hospitals, schools and prisons. Private consortia are contracted to design, build and manage a development (usually for around 25 years); the public authority then leases the building and service.

SEE *Social, ethical and environmental* represents a way of categorising a set of impacts. Most often used by socially responsible investors.

Sustainability Throughout the guide, the term *sustainability* refers to the triple bottom line of economic, social and environmental performance. Corporate social responsibility (CSR) is the business community's response to the challenges presented by sustainability.

SRI *Socially responsible investment* represents a type of investment that combines financial objectives with a commitment to social, environmental and ethical concerns. Institutional investors increasingly have specially selected SRI funds, managed via a process of negative screening and/or positive engagement.

Selected issues glossary

This list identifies some of the sustainability (the triple bottom line of economic, social and environmental performance) issues that might be relevant to property and construction companies. Some of the issues are very specific (eg crime prevention) and others are extremely broad in their nature (eg urban regeneration). Some, such as corporate governance, occur at the corporate level and some are specific to individual projects (eg nuisance). An analysis of existing sustainability reports within these industries, current issues investigated by SRI and mainstream investors, and a variety of other relevant literature. This list is by no means intended to be exhaustive, as there will be many more issues of relevance to the sustainability of companies and/or projects in the property and construction sectors.

Each issue may present both a risk and an opportunity as a result of either negative or positive impacts on the environment, economy or society.

Accessibility	Inclusive access to facilities (including access by disabled people, older people and children), wayfinding, access to public transport and respecting and responding to the needs of diverse user groups.
Affordable housing	The inclusion of a decent proportion of lower cost dwellings within wider developments.
Archaeology	The impacts of development activities on any ancient remains or artefacts that may be discovered on-site and to the impact on nearby ancient monuments. Appropriate assessments and site surveys should be undertaken at the planning stage, in order to minimise impact during construction.
Biodiversity	The range of wildlife (plants and animals) on or around a site that may be affected by development activities. Wildlife includes both protected and invasive species. Appropriate assessments and site surveys should be undertaken at the planning stage so as to minimise impact during construction.
Bribery and corruption	Conflicts of interest, fraud, insider dealing, the giving and receiving of gifts or bribes, and "whistle blowing" policies to expose such practices.
Charitable giving	Financial donations made to charitable organisations and sponsorship activities.
Community investment	The allocation of staff time or building space to community initiatives and the provision of physical community facilities on a long-term basis.
Community involvement	Communicating with and involving local residents, schools and businesses in the design and construction process, to ensure that they feel a sense of ownership in the development outcomes.
Community regeneration	The creation of more vibrant and cohesive communities through partnerships between property and construction companies, and local educational bodies, health organisations, and community-based institutions, to improve the social services and quality of life for people living in an area.
Corporate governance	The constitution of a company's board of directors and committee structures, in line with the requirements of the Combined Code of Corporate Governance (see Appendix 2 part 2).
Crime prevention	The design of buildings and environments to reduce the scope for crime and anti-social behaviour, which includes partnerships with the police or local youth groups/charities.
Customer satisfaction	Efforts to measure and improve customer care and quality of service provision, which might involve occupiers, purchasers, construction clients, the public or others.
Design/build quality and distinctiveness	Ensuring that developments provide a good quality built environment in the long term, championing inclusive and aesthetic design.
Disaster planning	Planning for the management of a major incident such as pollution, extreme weather or terrorist attacks.
Economic regeneration	Measures to attract businesses to locate in an area, create new jobs, and increase the number of visitors, customers or tenants.
Emissions to air	Discharges of pollutants to the atmosphere, including SOx, NOx, particulates, "greenhouse gases" such as CFCs and CO_2.
Emissions to land	Discharges of polluting substances to land, and creation of contamination. Primarily refers to spillages of hazardous substances such as fuel, oils and chemicals.
Emissions to water	Discharges to polluting substances to water, including silt, oils and chemicals.
Employee satisfaction	Employees' perceptions of the company, as measured through surveys and ratings, and corporate initiatives to attract and retain high-calibre staff.
Employment policies	Policies affecting a range of issues including remuneration and benefits, flexible working arrangements, training and skills development, and employee representation.
Energy use	All activities involving energy consumption (from different fuel types) across the range of a company's activities. Energy used within buildings can be significantly reduced through thoughtful design practices.

Selected issues glossary

Equal opportunities	Diversity and equality of opportunity through recruitment and ongoing employment policies, covering gender, ethnic origin, disability, age, religion and sexual orientation.	Nuisance	Anything interfering with the enjoyment of a person's premises constitutes as a nuisance. Key activities for construction and property companies are noise, vibration, dust, and mud.
Health and safety	Policies and management procedures to minimise accidents and personal injuries, and ensure the working environment does not have a detrimental impact on the longer-term health of employees, suppliers and customers.	Office resource efficiency	Minimising the waste of energy, water and materials, resulting from activities undertaken at administrative offices (as opposed to development or property sites).
Historical liabilities	Issues arising from the past uses of the land or buildings, such as contaminated land remediation or asbestos removal.	Political donations	Financial payments or donations made directly to political parties or indirectly to politically active bodies.
Human rights	Refers to a range of issues, including preventing discrimination, upholding political freedom and protecting people from inhumane conduct. Often related to labour conditions, human rights violations are often connected with developing countries, especially those where labour markets are not well regulated.	Quality of open spaces	Ensuring that open civic spaces and green spaces are of good quality, provide enjoyable and aesthetic design, and meet the needs of wide-ranging user groups.
		Stakeholder consultation	The identification of groups or individuals affected by, or with an interest in, a company's activities, and the methods used to identify their concerns and initiate open dialogue.
Innovation	The use of, and support for, new technologies and production processes in order to achieve business benefits.	Supply chain management (SCM)	A company's commitment to integrating sustainability issues into the selection and management of suppliers and contractors, eg ensuring suppliers are paying at least minimum wage levels.
Job creation	The creation of new employment opportunities, possibly by means of partnerships with other organisations.		
KPIs	The use of key performance indicators to measure a company's performance, and benchmark internally and externally across a range of issues, including sustainability.	Sustainable design/ life-cycle assessment	The consideration of the environmental and social impacts of a development throughout its entire life-span, from "cradle to grave". It requires a stewardship approach to minimise the negative environmental impacts associated with a buildings construction, operation, maintenance and eventual deconstruction.
Labour availability and sourcing	Relates to the ease with which suitably skilled employees can be recruited and whether such employees can and have been found in the locality of the development project.		
		Sustainable timber procurement	Purchasing timber and timber products from well-managed sources that are recognised accredited and can provide robust evidence of the point of origin. Several internationally recognised schemes exist such as the Forest Stewardship Council (FSC).
Land use	The amount of land that is taken by the development activities and whether the development occurs on previously developed brownfield land or on land that has not been previously developed. Such greenfield land is generally considered to be worthy of protection.		
		Transport	Measures taken to improve accessibility by sustainable transport (eg public transport, cycling and walking). If private cars are required, for employees to travel together when possible and to plan journeys to minimise mileage, and use of alternatives such as video conferencing when possible.
Management systems	Formal mechanisms in place for managing issues such as organisational quality, environmental impacts, health and safety, or employee development. Systems can be accredited to recognised standards such as ISO 14001, OHAS 18001, and ISO 9001 (see Appendix 2).		
		Waste	Minimising the wastes produced by company activities and ensuring that disposal options are considered from a sustainability perspective by considering the social, environmental and economic cost of reusing, recycling, recovery of energy or disposing to landfill.
Materials	Procurement and use of sustainable materials (eg certified timber), minimising use of virgin materials (aggregates), materials with high embodied energy or which do not break down in the natural environment (eg PVC, HCFC), minimising transportation, and applying the waste hierarchy (see below).		
		Water use	Water consumption levels and the measures used to control and reduce usage (eg water-efficient taps and flush systems, rainwater harvesting, and greywater recycling).

1 Introduction

This chapter establishes the background and purpose of the guide, identifies the target audiences, and contains instructions as to its use.

Throughout the guide, the term *sustainability* refers to the triple bottom line of economic, social and environmental performance. Corporate social responsibility (CSR) is the business community's response to the challenges presented by sustainability.

1.1 WHY USE THIS GUIDE

Socially responsible investment (SRI) is one of the fastest growing investment approaches as pension fund trustees recognise their responsibilities as shareholders, and personal investors seek to invest in line with their moral values or risk assessments. Social, ethical or environmental (SEE) factors are increasingly being accepted as having the potential to affect financial performance, and SRI is gradually moving away from negative screening towards proactive engagement over sustainability performance. More information about SRI can be obtained from the UK Social Investment Forum, <www.uksif.org.uk>.

Few investors, however, have developed methods for incorporating a measure of performance into financial analysis of industry sectors, such as property (real estate) or construction.

There are signs that the mainstream investment community is taking greater interest in the emerging evidence linking sustainability performance to long-term financial performance.

Katherine Garrett-Cox, chief investment officer of Morley Fund Management, says:

> *In our view, companies that combine good governance and corporate responsibility are better positioned for long-term success, so it is in our interests to use our influence as shareholders to promote good practice among the companies in which we are invested.... While only a small proportion of our funds are run on SRI criteria we believe we should use the insights gained from SRI research to engage constructively with all the companies whose shares we own.*

Indeed, listed companies are required to disclose information about the risks and opportunities they face, including future liabilities arising from changing operating conditions. Examples of recent developments include:

- Corporate governance – revisions to the Combined Code on Corporate Governance 27 (July 2003), which incorporates principles from:
    - Smith Guidance on Audit Committees (January 2003)
    - Higgs Report (January 2003)
    - Turnbull Guidance on Internal Control (September 1999)
- Company Law Review – Modernising Company Law (White Paper, July 2002); which led to the draft Regulations on the Operating and Financial Review and Directors' Report [36] (May 2004).

A growing number of companies across all sectors are responding by producing separate detailed reports on their environmental and/or social performance. However, they are being criticised for failing to integrate the key messages in their standard communications with (mainly mainstream) investors, who need to know which sustainability issues are most relevant to their businesses and why (both mainstream and SRI investors).

Background research conducted into the reporting practices of the property and construction industries, undertaken to inform the drafting of this guide suggests that, while companies in these industries are mirroring the general trend of issuing sustainability reports, they are not being transparent about the process by which they have identified the issues to report against and what impact these issues could have on their bottom line.

There also appear to be significant disparities between the sustainability issues that individual property and construction companies are reporting against and those that certain investors are asking questions about. Appendix 1 provides the key facts about corporate social, ethical and environmental performance, reporting and SRI.

There is therefore a need for sector-specific guidance to identify those sustainability issues that are most

1 Introduction

relevant to property and construction, and to illustrate how the issues might differ according to the particular characteristics of the sub-sector and the individual company.

This guide will inform:

- property and construction companies about the processes they can employ to identify sustainability issues that are most relevant to their businesses, and to communicate them effectively to the financial community
- mainstream and SRI investors in their investigations of sustainability performance among property and construction companies, and provide a standard against which to evaluate non-financial disclosure of such companies.

1.2 WHO SHOULD USE THIS GUIDE

Investing in tomorrow's company is specifically targeted at:

- companies in the property (real estate) and construction industries*; commercial property developers and investors, house-builders and all companies involved in construction activities
- investment companies – both mainstream investors and those involved in SRI.

* including the FTSE categorisation for the Real Estate and the Construction and Building Materials industrial sectors.

Within these organisations, the guidance will benefit the following:

- property and construction companies:
    - executive and non-executive directors
    - sustainability/CSR managers
    - investor relations and corporate communications officers
- investment community:
    - buy and sell side analysts
    - fund managers
    - pension fund trustees
    - corporate financiers/investment bankers.

This guidance has been developed with specific reference to the UK policy context but it should also be useful to companies operating in other countries.

1.3 HOW TO USE THIS GUIDE

Instructions on how to use the guide are included in each chapter, and distinctions drawn between the two target audiences.

The guidance is not intended to be prescriptive, so all users should use the concepts and ideas to help them refine their sustainability communications. *Investing in tomorrow's company* complements the use of other guidelines such as the OFR *Practical guidance to directors* [36]. It may be useful to property and construction companies in identifying which information is relevant for inclusion in their OFRs.

Table 1 *Comparison between* Investing in tomorrow's company *and the* OFR Practical guidance for directors

CIRIA C636 *Investing in tomorrow's company*	Operating and financial review – practical guidance for directors
Case studies and examples from the property and construction sectors	Spans across all industries
Focused on sustainability (ie environmental, social and economic performance)	Includes a very broad spectrum of information, only some of which will relate to social or environmental performance
Covers the wide spectrum of communications between property and construction companies and the investment community (mainstream and SRI)	Limited to preparation of the OFR
Targeted at both companies and the investment community, and could be applied by a much broader spectrum of employees	Targeted specifically at company directors

2 What to communicate

This chapter illustrates the way investors make investment decisions, highlights the need for companies to employ a systematic process in identifying their most relevant sustainability issues, and shows, through a series of hypothetical case studies, how such issues may differ between apparently similar companies.

2.1 UNDERSTANDING HOW INVESTORS MAKE DECISIONS

To maximise the effectiveness of sustainability communications with their investors, companies need first to understand the investment decision-making process. Figure 1 (overleaf) provides a simplified illustration of an approach a fund manager might take before deciding whether to buy, sell or hold any particular stock and where providing sustainability information might influence this process.

Essentially, all equity investors try to predict a company's future earnings and worth in order to determine which are the best stocks to buy to fulfil their mandate. While there is a wide range of financial models and valuation techniques, all investors focus on the balance between risk and return, and on the company's strategic positioning to benefit from changing market conditions. SRI analysts often take a long-term view, whereas mainstream analysts typically have short- to medium-term horizons.

2.2 DEFINING THE BOUNDARIES OF "RELEVANCE"

Effective sustainability communications between companies and their investors depend upon describing links between sustainability issues and financial performance. What is relevant to the business is ultimately of relevance to investors, whose interests are aligned with business success.

Table 2 *Examples of links between sustainability and business success among the property and construction sectors*

Factors affecting business success	Sustainable examples
Something that has a quantifiable impact on the company's future balance sheet, eg it affects: • costs • liabilities • value • the cost of capital.	Environmental taxation affects costs for property and construction industries. Examples include: • climate change levy • escalating landfill tax • aggregates tax. Risks such as climate change can affect liabilities for property and construction companies. Examples include: • increased maintenance caused by weathering • increased insurance premiums. If institutions become less inclined to pay for properties with poor environmental or social credentials, there will be a negative adjustment of yields, affecting the valuation of existing properties and the price of new acquisitions. In times of economic downturn, job creation may become a critical consideration for banks financing the capital costs of new developments.
Something that can have an effect on the company's market share or market positioning, ie revenue-generating capacity.	Property and construction companies that focus solely on greenfield development, or those that exclude mixed-use developments or regeneration projects, might be restricting their potential for sustaining and further growing market share.
Something that can affect the company's intangible value, such as brand, reputation, employee retention or innovation.	Skilled labour can be in short supply in the construction industry, so implementing effective employment policies may become essential to attracting and retaining a skilled labour force. Commercial property and house-building companies are competing in a fierce market where reputation and brand play an increasingly important role, ie brand exposure by the company name and logos appearing on site hoardings etc.

2 What to communicate

Investment idea or theme
eg Landfill Directive

Analysis against others:
- sector peers
- other sectors

Quantitative financial analysis

Assess the likely financial impact of the idea or theme on the company's earnings using valuation techniques such as discounted cashflow analysis.

The level of company growth and yield are also assessed, as is the company's profile to risk.

Example
Increased transport and landfill costs for hazardous wastes have the potential to add 5 per cent to a company's operating costs.

Qualitative analysis

Analyse the quality of company management and its ability to:
- foresee and respond to risks and opportunities posed
- formulate viable ideas and implement effective strategies

This is informed by face-to-face company meetings and also by assessing historic earnings to determine the effectiveness of past strategies (where possible this is input into the quantitative analysis).

Example
A company invests heavily in remediation techniques for dealing with contaminated land, to minimise the creation of hazardous wastes.

Investment recommendation

Made by analyst to the fund manager based on whether the company is over- or under-valued by the market:
- buy/sell/hold.

Optional SRI/ethical assessment
- Negative screening
- Positive engagement

Investment decision
made by the fund manager

Sources of information

Mainstream (traditional) sector analysts view information from a range of sources:
- sell side analysts make stock recommendations
- SRI analysts provide information on social, ethical and environmental (SEE) themes and governance issues
- strategists provide information on macro-economic issues, eg interest rates, sector allocations, job data, oil price, forthcoming legislation
- newsflow, eg political announcements.

Communication opportunities
- Company trading updates and results (annual report and accounts and OFRs)
- Environmental, sustainability, CSR reports
- Meetings and presentations to analysts.

Further information

Not necessarily related to financial performance.
- Negative screening may be implemented if the sector or company is involved in an activity that is not socially, ethically or environmentally acceptable, eg arms, tobacco, controversial dam-building.
- Positive shareholder engagement may be used to encourage companies across all sectors to enhance their business performance by addressing governance and SEE issues.

Communication opportunities
- Environmental, sustainability, CSR reports
- meetings and presentations to analysts.

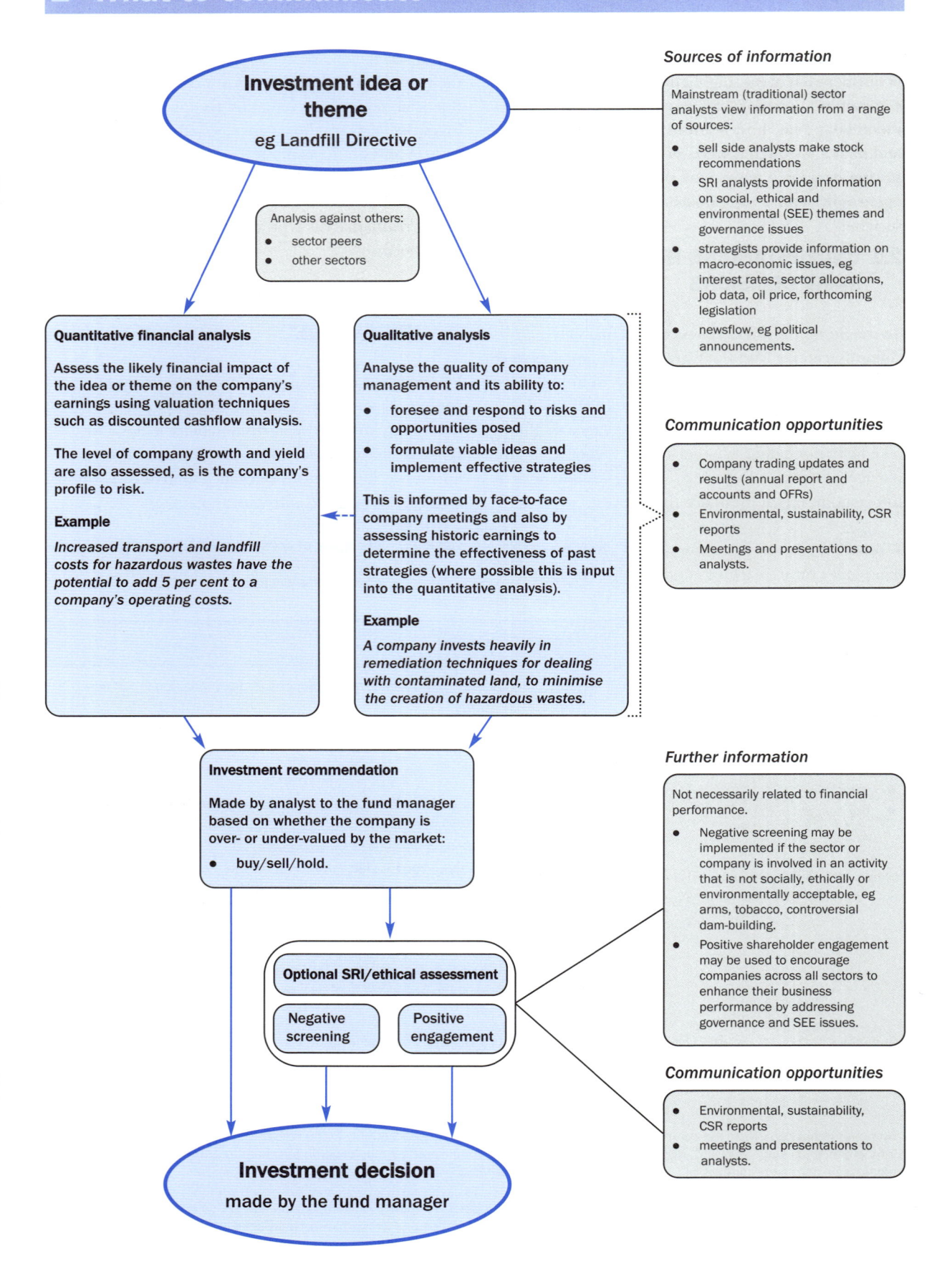

Figure 1 *An example of how investors make decisions. Note: this process will vary between companies*

2 What to communicate

Identifying the risks that might affect shareholder value is a pre-requisite of compliance with *Turnbull guidance* and the revised *Combined code of corporate governance*[27], which states that "the board should maintain a sound system of internal control to safeguard shareholders' investment and the company's assets". Sustainability issues, encompassing social, ethical, environmental and economic matters, should be embedded in the process for implementing such guidance. Such issues might represent business, operational, financial and other risks impacting on a company's ability to achieve its objectives.

When considering sustainability risks and opportunities, it is important to consider the stage of the development process that companies are involved in. Figure 2 illustrates these stages and provides some examples of potentially relevant sustainability issues.

For example:

- property and construction companies should find the diagram helpful during their initial discussions about sustainability
- investors may use the diagram as a starting point to inform their sector-based approaches to engagement and research on property and construction companies.

Appendix 2 provides a more extensive list of sustainability issues that may be relevant to property and construction sectors.

Table 3 provides some top tips for companies to identify and communicate sustainability issues.

Table 3 *Top tips when identifying the most relevant sustainability issues*

Do	Don't
Prioritise a small number of the most relevant sustainability issues and explain their relevance.	End up with a long list of issues with no indication of their relevance.
Consider both risks and opportunities (eg improved competitiveness).	Consider just past events without predicting future conditions.
Prioritise the risks identified by the company's mainstream risk registers and management procedures (ie Turnbull guidance requirements).	Assume an issue is relevant simply because certain investors are asking questions about it.
Establish the effect of issues on the company's bottom line and quantify short/medium/long-term cost benefits.	Use sustainability jargon, especially when communicating with mainstream investors.
Briefly identify issues that are less relevant to the company and be prepared to demonstrate why they are not relevant.	Conclude a particular issue is not relevant simply because insufficient information is available, or communicate about an issue just because information about it is easily obtained.

2 What to communicate

Relevant issues
- Sustainable materials selection
- Accessibility
- Affordable housing
- Sustainable design/life-cycle assessment

Questions from investors
- How are risks and opportunities identified and managed on site, both directly and with the supply chain?
- Do adequate training and awareness programmes for site workers exist on environmental management and H&S?
- How many injuries, fatalities and incidents occurred in the past year and how many fines has the company incurred?
- How does the company influence clients regarding sustainability issues?

Relevant issues
- Waste management
- Emissions to air, land and water
- Nuisance and community liaison
- Health and safety

Questions from investors
- Does the company have control over the design and specification of new build, redevelopment or refurbishment?
- What community consultation techniques does the company employ at the early planning stage to avoid unnecessary delay from opposition?
- For what types of properties does the company have design responsibility and what opportunities are there for integrating sustainability features?
- What sustainability standards does the company set itself as a minimum at the design stage (eg BREEAM[3], CEEQUAL[5], Secured by design[24] etc)?

Central diagram — Business management:
- Sustainability policy and governance
- Investment/development strategy
- Business ethics/code of conduct
- Human resources
- Communication
- Marketing
- Accountability and transparency
- Office resource efficiency: waste, energy etc
- Corporate community affairs
- Supply chain management
- Corporate governance
- Financial performance

Stages (cyclical): Design/planning → Construction → Operation management → Refurbishment (see design/planning issues) → Demolition (see construction issues) → Site acquisition

Questions from investors
- Does the company have an investment portfolio? If so, does it consist of multi-let properties over which the company retains more managerial control?
- Is the company managing certain properties as a result of PFI contracts?
- What types of properties are in the portfolio (eg retail, office, industrial) and what opportunities do they provide in terms of integrating sustainability?
- Does the company incorporate any standard lease clauses to address sustainability risks at tenant-controlled properties?
- How does the company maximise efficiencies in its own office occupation?

Relevant issues
- Land use
- Biodiversity
- Historical liabilities, eg asbestos
- Economic regeneration

Questions from investors
- Does the company buy land to be retained for future development?
- Is the company's land bank strategically in line with UK Government policy on regeneration and targeted development areas?
- Does the company use a sustainability checklist to assess sites before acquisition?

Relevant issues
- Resource use: energy, water etc
- Contract services
- Security and crime prevention
- Job creation

Figure 2 Sustainability issues according to the stage of the development process. Note: the questions are not necessarily linked to the issues shown

2 What to communicate

2.3 DEMONSTRATING A SYSTEMATIC APPROACH

It is important, particularly when communicating with SRI investors, for companies to be transparent about how they have identified particular sustainability issues, why these are felt to be the most relevant and why others have been excluded. All these facts will help to demonstrate a systematic approach to managing and communicating sustainability.

As suggested in Section 2.2, identifying sustainability risks and opportunities forms an integral part of standard risk management and corporate governance practices. In addition, emerging principles of good practice exist that apply more specifically to managing sustainability risks and opportunities. Figure 3 highlights some examples of these, a combination of which would validate the process employed by property and construction companies. It is not intended to be prescriptive, since the process will vary according to corporate culture and the maturity of sustainability management within any one company. Figure 3 should be used by:

- property and construction companies to establish and refine the processes they employ to identify their most relevant sustainability issues. They should inform SRI investors of the steps taken to demonstrate the robustness of their approach
- SRI investors to evaluate property and construction companies' approach to identifying their most relevant sustainability issues, by referring to the processes outlined in the figure.

It is important to recognise that the relevance of sustainability issues will change over time, so the process of identifying and prioritising them will be a continuing one. Outcomes need to be regularly reviewed in the light of:

- changing societal norms, stakeholder perceptions and inherent risks
- tightening regulatory framework
- corporate improvements in sustainability performance
- increasing sophistication of technologies and science-based solutions
- evolving best practice
- media and NGO-related campaigns
- evolving company characteristics (for example new investment strategies).

2.4 HYPOTHETICAL CASE STUDIES

No two companies are the same. It is conceivable that property or construction companies will conclude that different sustainability issues are those most relevant to their businesses. Some key variables that will affect the relevance of issues for companies in these sectors include:

- the type of activities undertaken, including the stage of the property process over which they have managerial control and the type of projects or properties in which they invest
- the type of contractual arrangements they have with tenants, clients and suppliers
- the geographical location of developments, investments and sites.

2 What to communicate

Business planning
eg board of directors, company secretariat, legal department, sustainability/CSR committee

- Several property and construction companies have developed their own code of conduct, core values, business ethics policy or customer charter.
- These often refer specifically to sustainability commitments for which the company could be held accountable.

← **Review central policies** and values to identify commitments with social, ethical or environmental implications.

- Energy Performance of Buildings Directive[10] (energy certificate required from January 2005).
- Sustainable Comunities Plan for affordable housing in Lonon and the South East[26] (Feb 2003).
- Landfill Directive[19] – reduction in landfill sites able to take hazardous waste from July 2004.

← **Forecast** future events based upon known facts (eg incoming legislation) and potential scenarios (eg market conditions).

- House-builders often report on land use, H&S and skills shortages.
- Contractors often report on waste management, H&S and community involvement.
- Property investors often report on whole-life costs, energy use, community investment and local economic regeneration.

← **Review** the most relevant **sustainability issues** against those identified by similar companies within the same peer group.

Identify the most relevant issues

Communications
eg corporate communications, investor relations, human resources, sustainability/CSR committee

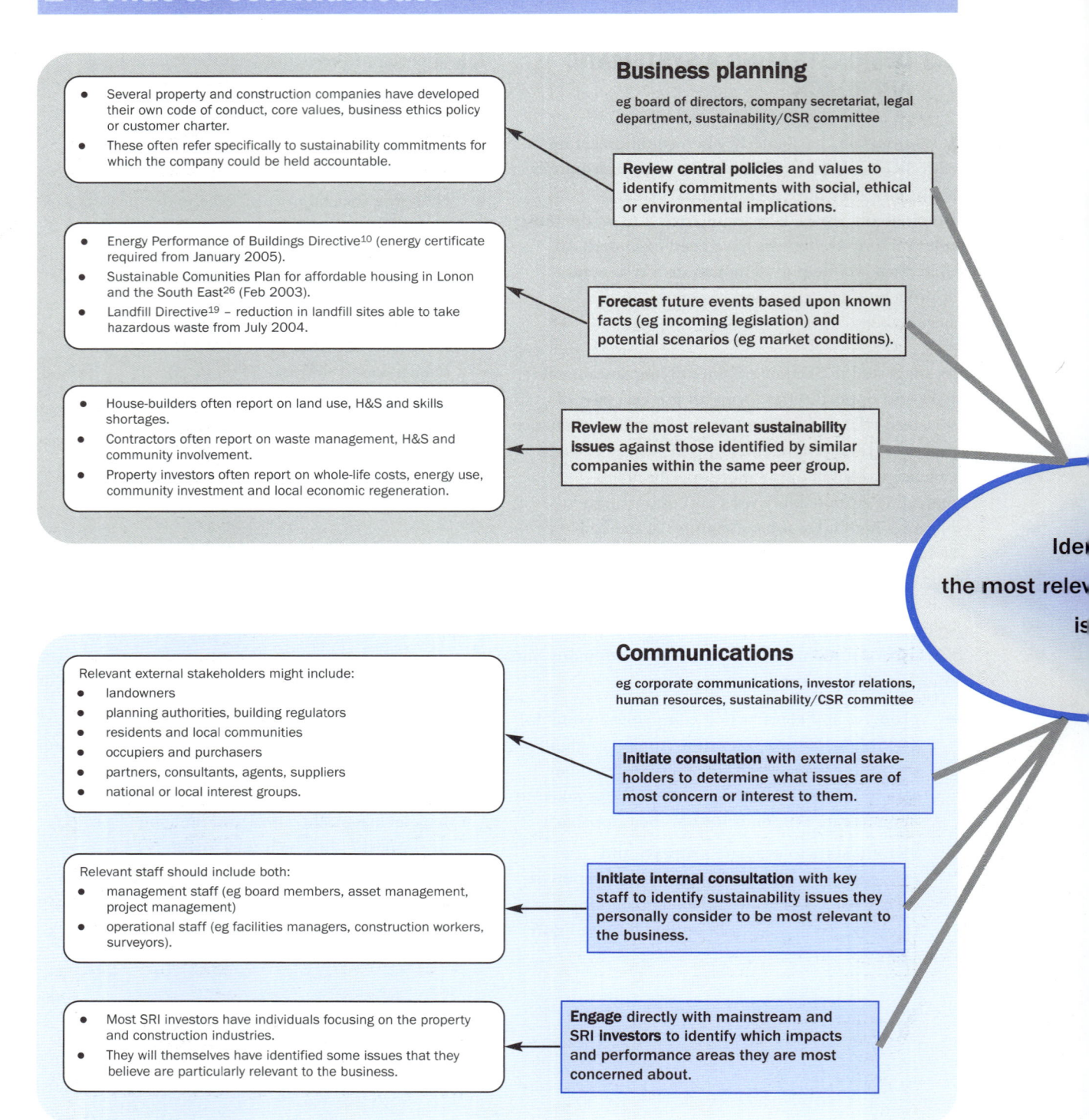

Relevant external stakeholders might include:
- landowners
- planning authorities, building regulators
- residents and local communities
- occupiers and purchasers
- partners, consultants, agents, suppliers
- national or local interest groups.

← **Initiate consultation** with external stakeholders to determine what issues are of most concern or interest to them.

Relevant staff should include both:
- management staff (eg board members, asset management, project management)
- operational staff (eg facilities managers, construction workers, surveyors).

← **Initiate internal consultation** with key staff to identify sustainability issues they personally consider to be most relevant to the business.

- Most SRI investors have individuals focusing on the property and construction industries.
- They will themselves have identified some issues that they believe are particularly relevant to the business.

← **Engage** directly with mainstream and SRI **investors** to identify which impacts and performance areas they are most concerned about.

Figure 3 *Example of a systematic approach.*
Note: companies can start at any point and follow their selected steps in any order

2 What to communicate

Risk management
eg audit committee, company secretariat, board of directors, finance, legal department

Review past events that have affected the company and more general trends that have affected the sector.
- Lengthy community protests at controversial development sites (eg Newbury Bypass, Manchester Airport).
- NGO campaigns on individual properties (eg illegal timber in government buildings).
- Fatalities on construction sites and railway operations.

Analyse how **sustainability issues** might **affect the markets** in which the company operates and thereby link to market share.
- The push for better public-sector procurement is raising environmental performance requirements for developers, civil engineering companies and landlords who wish to secure government clients (eg agencies, departments, local authorities).

Integrate **sustainability** into the **risk management** process, using a systematic methodology to evaluate relative risk significance.
- Several property and construction companies have ISO 14001[17] accreditation at individual sites, which is based on a systematic evaluation of environmental risks.
- The same should be done across social and economic risks at corporate and/or site level.

Operations
eg acquisition and disposal, development, asset management, administration

Review the core business activities to identify potential areas of impact on economy, society and environment.
- Existing tools and guidance can help:
- BREEAM[3], CEEQUAL[5].
- WWF/Insight One Million Sustainable Homes initiative[14].
- Sustainable Code for Buildings etc[25].

Establish the **potential links** between **different issues**, in particular environmental and social issues with financial performance.
- There are direct cost savings to be achieved through eco-efficiencies (eg energy and water savings or reduced waste to landfill).
- Social issues such as employee morale have been directly correlated to customer/supplier satisfaction and help generate higher profits.

Seek specialist guidance on the sustainability implications of the business strategy and core activities.
- Advisers should understand the property development and investment process.
- They should be sustainability experts able to identify the risks/opportunities that exist at both the corporate level (eg investment strategy) and the site/property level (eg land contamination).

2 What to communicate

Company HB1

Key characteristics

- HB1 is a large-scale developer that has a predominantly brownfield, eight-year land bank. The company is experiencing rapid growth.
- The company specialises in urban renewal projects.
- Employee turnover has traditionally been very low and the company has recently introduced a graduate recruitment programme.
- In recent years the company has been associated with several water pollution incidents, primarily by allowing silt to flow into adjacent watercourses.

Hypothetical external context

- Planning consents are more readily given to developers providing mixed-use, mixed-tenure developments within easy reach of existing infrastructure and amenities.
- The Environment Agency has visited several sites managed by the company and has issued an abatement notice on one site where significant risks were identified.
- Industry benchmarking has been undertaken regarding the design of public open space, highlighting the best and worst performers.

Sustainability communications

HB1's sustainability communications with investors highlight the following:

- **Quality of open public spaces:** HB1 has sponsored the development of good practice guidelines and adopts this on all developments.
- **Community regeneration:** how well-designed mixed-use developments can help rejuvenate local communities and reduce crime.
- **Water pollution:** HB1 records and reports on water pollution incidents and near misses. The company ensures that all sub-contractors are trained to minimise the likelihood of an incident occurring.
- **Employee training:** the company is recognised as an investor in people and implements an ongoing personal development programme for staff.

Company HB2

Key characteristics

- HB2 is a medium-size house-builder with a mixed land bank of brownfield and greenfield sites.
- Some of the brownfield locations are in traditionally deprived inner-city areas that suffer from high crime rates.
- The board is committed to sustainability issues and has a policy of going beyond compliance wherever practical.

Hypothetical external context

- In the previous 12 months three NGOs have asked about the company's sustainable timber procurement strategy.
- Increasingly customers are showing an interest in the environmental performance of their homes, particularly energy efficiency, linked to the rising cost of fuel.
- The UK Government has set a target of 60 per cent of all new residential development to be built on brownfield land.

Sustainability communications

HB2's sustainability communications with investors highlight the following:

- **Crime prevention:** the company uses the principle of "secured by design"[24] and meets with police local architectural liaison officers on all projects.
- **Sustainable procurement policy:** HB2 has a sustainable materials policy, which includes timber from certified sources and preference for recycled timber.
- **Land use:** HB2 has a commitment to exceed the government's target of 60 per cent of new developments built on previously developed land.
- **Customer satisfaction:** post-occupancy evaluations are undertaken, which include energy performance.

Company HB3

Key characteristics

- HB3 is a smaller building company employing 50 direct staff. The company subcontracts much of the work undertaken on site.
- Developments are generally towards the high end of the housing market, traditionally in suburban and rural areas. Many types of designs are used.
- The company is reluctant to become involved with brownfield sites because of the perceived financial risks associated with possible contamination.

Hypothetical external context

- The Health and Safety Executive has visited several company sites in the past year and is particularly focused on the risks of working at height.
- The construction programme was delayed by local protestors at one large rural development.
- New waste legislation and increasing taxation, such as the Landfill Directive and landfill tax, threaten to increase the company's costs significantly.
- Planning authorities are increasingly interested in how developers can demonstrate how their designs can help encourage biodiversity.

Sustainability communications

HB3's sustainability communications with investors highlight the following:

- **Safety:** initiatives to ensure safe working conditions of all employees, including training, demonstrations and any Health and Safety Executive-reportable incidents or near misses.
- **Waste:** KPIs are used, including the amount of waste produced per dwelling and the percentage of waste that was recycled.
- **Biodiversity:** how species and habitats have been conserved, created and enhanced by company developments.
- **Community liaison:** the company has a policy to consult with neighbours at the planning stage and during construction. Site managers are tasked with reducing complaints and all sites are registered with the Considerate Constructors Scheme.

Figure 4   *Hypothetical case studies: house-builders*

2 What to communicate

Company C1

Key characteristics

- C1 is a large construction company with international interests, employing more than 40 000 staff worldwide.
- The company chiefly works on large-scale projects, including retail, residential, healthcare and utilities.
- In the UK the company is involved in several PFI projects that involve the design, construction, maintenance and operation of the building.
- C1 operates an international code of conduct that goes beyond legal compliance on employee relations, business ethics and the environment.

⬇

Hypothetical external context

- In the past NGOs have questioned the company's previous involvement in dam-building projects.
- Increasing demands from clients, including government, to incorporate sustainability features into designs.
- Investors have previously questioned the company on its labour conditions and employee welfare policies across its global operations.

⬇

Sustainability communications

C1's sustainability communications with investors highlight the following:

- **Resource use** (energy and water): including the operation of facilities designed and built by the company.
- **Sustainability impact assessments:** have resulted in the company choosing not to get involved with certain projects that have negative social or environmental effects.
- **Sustainable design and construction:** includes communicating the results of assessment methodologies such as BREEAM[3] for buildings and CEEQUAL[5] for civil engineering projects.
- **Human rights:** including labour conditions and local labour sourcing.

Company C2

Key characteristics

- C2 is a large construction company operating exclusively in the UK.
- It acts as a managing agent, with sub-contractors providing all site operatives on C2-managed sites.
- Sub-contractors use large numbers of foreign site operatives, particularly from eastern Europe.
- The company is involved in several large-scale urban regeneration projects across the UK.
- C2 has recognised management systems in place for environment, quality and health and safety issues.

⬇

Hypothetical external context

- Local regeneration partnerships usually require high environmental and social standards, including engagement with local communities and other stakeholders
- C2 has been prosecuted for several health and safety infringements, including one fatality.
- Most sub-contractors are small companies that may lack resources to develop their own sustainability strategies
- Recent waste legislation has resulted in a doubling of the cost of some company waste streams.

⬇

Sustainability communications

C2's sustainability communications with investors highlight the following:

- **Stakeholder consultation:** taking stakeholders' concerns on board to deliver the most sustainable regeneration outcome.
- **Health and safety:** recording staff training provided and monitoring against incidents occurring.
- **Supply chain management:** appropriate training provided to ensure that all site operatives are aware of, and understand, relevant procedures.
- **Waste management:** total waste produced per square metre constructed and proportion sent to landfill.

Company C3

Key characteristics

- C3 is a medium-sized civil engineering contractor employing around 600 direct staff.
- The company has grown rapidly, mainly through acquisitions.
- C3 operates across the UK.
- Many of the company's clients are government departments such as the Highways Agency on road building and maintenance and the Environment Agency on waterways and coastal defence.

⬇

Hypothetical external context

- Government clients require main contractors to have rigorous systems in place to manage environmental and health and safety risks on site.
- Sustainability issues can account for up to 20 per cent of tenders.
- C3 is engaged in long-term contractual agreements and frameworks with several clients.
- A sharp drop in skilled tradesmen entering the construction sector has been experienced in recent years.

⬇

Sustainability communications

C3's sustainability communications with investors highlight the following:

- **Integrated management system:** implemented company-wide and certified to ISO 14001[17], OHAS 18001[21], ISO 9001[18] and incorporates social issues such as working conditions. C3 publicly communicates performance relating to all areas of the IMS and makes its sustainability policy available.
- **Customer satisfaction:** questions clients in detail about how well the company met the brief; also undertakes post-occupancy evaluation with the users of all buildings.
- **Labour availability and sourcing:** operates apprenticeship programmes to help young employees gain further skills.

Figure 5   *Hypothetical case studies: construction contractors*

2 What to communicate

Company P1

Key characteristics

- P1 is a commercial property investor and developer with investments located throughout the UK.
- The company's portfolio comprises of retail, industrial and offices.
- It provides accommodation to several large central and regional government departments and is seeking to expand its services to other public-sector clients.
- P1 has only 200 direct employees and outsources or sub-contracts significant responsibilities such as day-to-day property management, cleaning, security, design, construction etc.

Hypothetical external context

- Leading UK cities are on amber alert for a terrorism attack. Government has urged companies to develop business continuity plans.
- The UK Government has recently relaunched its green procurement policy, announcing that all public-sector procurement must comply with rigorous environmental assessments.
- Following recent NGO campaigns, the government is particularly concerned to ensure that any timber used within its buildings is sourced from sustainably managed forests.

Sustainability communications

P1's sustainability communications with investors highlight the following:

- **Security:** meticulous security planning by the company will prevent or mitigate the risk of a terrorism attack.
- **Environmental management:** commitment to achieve ISO 14001[17] will secure market share for public-sector contracts.
- **Supply chain management:** integrating social and environmental standards in SCM practices will prevent a reputational risk arising as a result of P1's suppliers' activities.
- **Political donations, bribery and corruption:** P1's exposure to public-sector clients and its extensive development programme requires openness and transparency to prevent reputational risk.

Company P2

Key characteristics

- P2 is a commercial property developer with no retained investment portfolio.
- The company specialises in developing high-quality business parks in edge-of-town locations across the UK and continental Europe.
- It undertakes both speculative and pre-let development and has a public mission statement to be "developer of choice" for all end-users of its buildings.
- The company's philosophy is publicly stated in core values that include innovation, integrity and leadership.
- P2 is a relatively young company and has fewer than 30 full-time employees.

Hypothetical external context

- Several regional development agencies have issued a sustainability checklist to assess sustainability performance of all developments within their region before granting planning permission.
- The EU has issued a Directive on the Energy Performance of Buildings[10], which will require every building, when constructed, sold or rented, to have a certificate based on its energy efficiency performance.
- Many planning authorities in the area where the company works favour planning applications incorporating environmental aspects, particularly features to encourage biodiversity.

Sustainability communications

P2's sustainability communications with investors highlight the following:

- **Design quality/distinctiveness and environmental design:** design distinctiveness is important to attract blue-chip clients. P2 has set a minimum standard of "Very good" BREEAM[3] rating for all new UK developments to help secure planning permission from the local economic development agency.
- **Ecology:** P2 monitors the impact that its developments have on wildlife and ecology, including habitat creation and use of sustainable drainage systems.
- **Employee satisfaction:** to retain existing staff and recruit the best young graduates, P2 promotes sustainability across employment policies and training and development.

Company P3

Key characteristics

- P3 is a commercial property investor with a portfolio of refurbished old industrial buildings converted into business centres, mostly in London and the South East.
- P3 undertakes no new development activity but actively manages most of its multi-let centres. It provides services to occupiers such as energy purchasing, recycling and insurance.
- Some of its properties are in deprived and run-down areas.
- The size of the portfolio means that P3 tends to have a proportion of its unoccupied space that is not rented.

Hypothetical external context

- The UK Government strongly advocates urban renewal and regeneration as a major focus for property development.
- The Mayor of London has issued an economic development strategy encouraging enterprise and job creation in deprived boroughs.
- P3's customers are small and medium-sized enterprises, mainly in the creative arts and charitable sectors, so several have a social or environmental remit.
- One in every five new jobs in London is in the creative industries.

Sustainability communications

P3's sustainability communications with investors highlight the following:

- **Sustainability policy:** the profile of P3's customers requires it to demonstrate excellent sustainability performance in order to retain high levels of customer satisfaction.
- **Community investment:** P3 can offer space at affordable rents to educational or arts/culture organisations, which in turn can lead to exposure to new potential customers and strengthen brand equity.
- **Economic regeneration:** through investment in deprived areas, P3 is creating local employment opportunities and reviving local communities, strengthening its own brand within the London economy.

Figure 6 *Hypothetical case studies: commercial property companies*

3 How to communicate

This chapter emphasises the role of communications within a robust sustainability management system, provides guidance on the development of a sustainability communications or investor relations strategy, and signposts the reader to more detailed good practice guidance in sustainability communications.

3.1 MEASURING, MONITORING AND MANAGING

It is often said that the best form of communication is through action. Those companies that spend time and resources on the practical implementation of sustainability, realigning their core business and managing their impacts, should already have a reputation for governance and good risk management. Communication alone cannot be a substitute for attentive management of the issues.

It is critical that the issues most relevant to the business are adequately identified, measured, monitored and managed before being communicated to investors. Detailed sustainability communications with investors should include evidence of such management activities since these demonstrate a robust approach to managing risks and maximising opportunities associated with sustainability. Indeed, those companies that view sustainability as purely a communication exercise expose themselves to reputational risk and accusations of "greenwash".

Table 4 summarises the purpose of measuring, monitoring and managing, and illustrates this with examples from property and construction. Appendix 2 provides further details of commonly used indicators, benchmarks and standards in property and construction sectors.

Table 4   *Measuring, monitoring and managing sustainability in property and construction activities*

Purpose	Property and construction examples
Measuring It is difficult to manage what is not being measured either quantitatively or qualitatively. After prioritising the sustainability issues most relevant to the business, suitable indicators should be identified against which the company's performance can be measured.	Examples of performance indicators might include: • affordable housing: percentage by number of dwellings built • climate change: $kgCO_2$ per unit of construction or by m^2 of floor area • energy use within buildings: kWh/m^2 • job creation: number of jobs created • waste sent to landfill during construction: m^3/£100 000. In selecting appropriate performance indicators, companies need to review which ones other companies in the sector are using or, where industry benchmarks already exist, to provide meaningful comparisons. Such metrics should be easy to calculate, easy to explain and understand, and recognisable.
Monitoring Measurements should be viewed in context. There are three main options: 1 Monitoring one's own performance over time	Examples of monitoring practices might include: • comparing energy consumption in one building year on year • comparing weight of waste to landfill per unit of construction across different sites. Property and construction companies should not be afraid to report against worsening performance, but should be able to provide reasons for it.
2 Monitoring one's own performance against that of similar organisations ("benchmarking").	• Comparing the ratings one company achieves under a particular standard (eg BREEAM or EcoHomes) with that achieved by peers. • In the property and construction industries, properties and projects are highly variable in size, nature and duration, making it difficult to compare like with like, even within one property type.
3 Monitoring one's own performance in the wider social, environmental and social context.	• Comparing the accident rate of one construction company as a percentage of the total workplace accidents in the UK construction sector in the most recent year. • Comparing the ethnic diversity of a company's workforce with that of UK workforce.
Managing The ultimate aim of measuring and monitoring one's performance is to improve it continuously through robust management procedures.	Examples of robust management procedures might include: • setting performance targets, eg a minimum BREEAM/EcoHomes/CEEQUAL rating • providing staff and supplier incentives for improved performance such as fewer H&S incidents on site • ensuring consistency across all sites by distributing documented sustainability procedures manuals and auditing compliance against them.

CIRIA C636

3 How to communicate

3.2 DEVELOPING A SUSTAINABILITY COMMUNICATIONS STRATEGY

Corporate sustainability communications should be carefully planned to ensure maximum effectiveness in affecting the decisions made by investors and other stakeholders. The following pointers might assist property and construction companies in planning their sustainability communications strategies:

- identify target audiences – distinguishing between mainstream, SRI investors and others – and prioritise them according to their influence and importance

- develop a focused communications programme both in terms of scope and approach (including clear actions, milestones and responsibilities) bearing in mind ways in which investors make investment decisions (see Figure 1)

- identify how sustainability issues comprise operational and financial risk (and related volatility) and how this may be managed, while also demonstrating to investors how sustainability issues add value to the business (eg reduce risk, improve brand etc)

- integrate sustainability issues into existing communication channels, such as presentations to analysts and the annual report and accounts (AR&A). This requires a proactive approach since investors may not be asking questions about sustainability, but it could benefit the company to inform them of its approach

- ensure that sustainability communications integrate with the company's brand and overall business objectives, such as the mission statement and core values

- consult with investors and other stakeholders regularly to get feedback on the company's approach to sustainability and use this to shape the future priorities. Build in some evaluation measures to determine whether the communication objectives remain appropriate and are being met over time.

Property and construction companies preparing their communications with investors should consider the following in Table 5.

Table 5 *Key considerations for communicating sustainability to investors*

Communication considerations	Property and construction examples
Make sure investors understand the big picture of how sustainability has shaped or affected the business strategy.	Those companies that have realigned their business to take advantage of the urban regeneration markets are ideally positioned to contribute to local social, environmental and economic sustainability. As a result, they may also be benefiting from tax incentives, government funding, relaxed planning frameworks and an enhanced reputation among stakeholders.
Inform investors of policy implementation at the level of individual properties and sites, and consider preparing project-specific sustainability communications, over and above corporate-wide reports.	There is a growing trend in these industry sectors for sustainability communications to relate specifically to individual investment properties and development sites. Shopping centres, for example, can play a major role in town centre management and community integration plans. They will have unique sustainability risks and opportunities that would best be captured in standalone sustainability reports.
Invite investors to events, meetings and presentations that are not primarily aimed at them but that demonstrate the company's approach to sustainability in practice.	Events of relevance to which investors might normally be invited include launch events and construction site open days. Clear messages of good practice in sustainability management can be effectively communicated alongside associated business benefits.
Do not be afraid of reporting on bad news as well as good, as this demonstrates a true commitment to transparency and willingness to learn from previous mistakes.	In the property and construction sectors, bad news could take the form of environmental incidents or fines, health and safety accidents or fatalities, or community disruption for cause of nuisance, among many other things. It will be important to ensure that the company is able to demonstrate how it has put in place effective management systems in response to the adverse event.

3 How to communicate

3.3 NON-FINANCIAL REPORTING

Company non-financial reporting requirements are continuously evolving. An important recent example is the draft regulation proposing that all quoted UK companies may be required to produce *Operating and financial reviews*[36] (OFRs) for financial years beginning on or after 1 January 2005. OFRs would need to include details of a company's objectives and strategies, and provide information on "a wide range of factors which may be relevant to an understanding of the business, such as information about employees, environmental matters and community and social issues". The regulation specifies that if a company reports nothing on these areas, then it must make an explicit statement to explain why this is the case.

Beyond this guidance, there are no strict rules in UK company law that apply to sustainability communications with investors. However, principles of good practice are emerging and Table 6 highlights some of these in relation to AR&As, standalone sustainability/CSR reports and company websites.

Table 6 *Sustainability communications with investors*

Annual reports and accounts, and operating and financial reviews	Good practice requires companies to cover sustainability in their AR&As. Indeed, some investors go so far as to vote against a company's AR&A if it does not include any such information. The AR&A is likely to be most useful in reaching mainstream investors. The Association of British Insurers (ABI) published disclosure guidelines on SRI in 2001[32], which many SRI investors have adopted as the minimum sustainability disclosures for such reports. They refer specifically to board responsibilities for social, ethical and environmental (SEE) matters, and to policies, procedures and verification – see Appendix 2. Such content will need to be balanced with *Guidance for directors* on the OFR[36] once the draft regulations are approved. The intended audience for OFRs are the owners of the company, so it seems appropriate for the OFR to be included within the AR&A.
Standalone sustainability reports	More detailed information on sustainability performance should also be included in separate sustainability reports, which are likely to be more useful vehicles for reaching SRI investors who may be more interested in the detail than mainstream investors. A large number of good practice sustainability reporting guidelines have emerged over the years, and references to the most high profile of these can be found in Appendix 2 part 2 of this guide. Such guidance requires standalone sustainability reports to cover the following key information: • vision and strategy (including a clear identification of the relevant sustainability issues) • company profile and report scope • governance structure and risk management systems (including stakeholder engagement programmes) • company performance against economic, social and environmental indicators.
Sustainability information on the company website	The use of the World Wide Web has dramatically increased for the purposes of sustainability reporting and in particular for providing detailed evidence to support statements made in the AR&A and standalone sustainability report. In general, the website might be more appropriate than the AR&A and the standalone sustainability report for the following types of information: • responses to surveys and questionnaires • detailed case studies of the company's approach in practice – eg sustainability implementation at individual development projects and investment properties • relevant policies and detailed assessment of progress against individual objectives and targets • archived information and previous years' reports.

3 How to communicate

Unavoidable overlap between these different communication vehicles may be minimised through clear signposting and cross-referencing tools.

3.4 COMMUNICATION MEDIA

There is a variety of other media in which sustainability information can, and should, be passed on to investors. Indeed, one of the best ways of gaining a complete picture of a company's approach is through face-to-face contact.

Integrating sustainability considerations into existing communication channels might involve a combination of the following:

- responses to investor questionnaires
- presentations to analysts
- site visits and tours
- annual investor relations days
- monitoring internet usage by investor organisations
- ongoing communications
    - correspondence/email
    - telephone conversations
    - integrating questions about non-financial performance within investor relations surveys.

Certain research agencies continue to make use of questionnaires for the creation and maintenance of their indices (eg FTSE4Good[44], Dow Jones Sustainability Indices[42] and so on). Companies that are transparent about their approach to sustainability will benefit from reducing the time required to respond to such questionnaires. They may also find it helpful to consider initiatives such as the London Stock Exchange's recently launched Corporate Responsibility Exchange[45] – an online tool allowing companies to fill out a single questionnaire (instead of many) and giving investors a single site where they can locate and analyse company data.

3.5 ASSURANCE AND VERIFICATION

The essence of good sustainability communications lies in a company's ability to validate its performance through independent verification and assurance. This may take the form of compliance with an externally certified standard (eg ISO 14001[17]; Investors in people[16]) as well as verification of the sustainability reports themselves against the following principles:

- **materiality**: does the report provide an account identifying and covering all the areas of performance that investors need to judge the organisation's sustainability performance?
- **completeness**: is the information complete and accurate enough to allow assessment and understanding of the organisation's performance in all these areas? Does the form of reporting facilitate inter-company comparisons to be drawn?
- **responsiveness**: has the organisation responded coherently and consistently to investors' concerns and interests?

To improve confidence in reporting, property and construction companies may consider commissioning independent assurance providers to verify their sustainability communications to investors, rather like the way that financial reports require independent auditing.

4 Conclusions

Companies in the property and construction sectors may find it helpful to improve their sustainability communications with investors by following the process that has been put forward in this guide. The process is cyclical, since effective communication with investors on sustainability issues is an ongoing objective. It requires companies to:

- understand how investors might make decisions and how providing sustainability information might influence this process
- identify and prioritise the key sustainability issues that are most relevant to their business using a systematic and comprehensive process, considering:
    - the stage of the property development, construction and investment process in which they are involved
    - the company's key characteristics and external context (policy issues and stakeholder concerns)
- link sustainability performance with financial performance in all communications with investors
- measure, monitor and manage the key sustainability issues effectively using appropriate measurement criteria and methodology
- consider inter-company comparison with similar companies, particularly in the ways they measure and report on specific sustainability issues
- develop a sustainability communications strategy appropriate for investors, considering both non-financial reporting requirements and other communication media. This should include careful design of the output, channel and communication flow in order to be effective
- obtain verification and assurance for key outputs so as to add credibility to the company's sustainability communications
- review the relevance of the sustainability issues selected on a continuing basis and reflect any new issues in the ongoing management systems and communication strategy.

The process described in this guide should benefit investors by providing:

- an introduction to the sustainability risks and opportunities that might be relevant to property and construction activities and an initial understanding of how these have the potential to affect business performance
- a means for evaluating the relevance of particular sustainability issues to property and construction companies
- a basis for comparing the sustainability communications of property and construction companies.

Appendix 1   Key facts

SRI is growing as investors increasingly recognise the importance of social, ethical and environmental performance:

- recent research shows that two-thirds of personal investors (65 per cent) are interested in having their money invested in a socially responsible way. Interest in ethical investment rises to three quarters (74 per cent) of those personal investors under the age of 45. The ethical fund market has grown faster than that of funds in general

- increasing numbers of pension funds are building social and environmental issues into their investment practice, with the trend set to continue strongly in the next few years

- in the UK, more than £120 billion has been invested in institutional and retail funds with active SRI policies, and over £100 billion has been invested by insurance companies seeking investments with lower social and environmental risks

- the total UK funds under management that can be classified as SRI has gown by around 50 per cent a year over the last few years.

The mainstream investment community is now taking an interest in the following ways:

- SRI analysts are increasingly engaging with their financial analyst colleagues on the investment risks and opportunities posed by certain social and environmental business practices. The contribution of non-financial performance to market value (in such areas as corporate governance, transparency and business ethics) is a particular issue following recent scandals in the United States

- mainstream investor engagement on social, ethical and environmental performance appears to be becoming much more widespread in the UK, with a focus on protecting shareholder value by integrating engagement on such issues with the mainstream corporate governance process, on the basis of informal dialogue and collaboration

- the Dow Jones sustainability index and the FTSE4Good index both appear to have performed in line with, or outperformed, the broader market averages, although the analysis depends heavily on the time period that is under consideration

- the conclusion from a study undertaken by the Institute of Business Ethics is that there is strong evidence to indicate that larger UK companies with codes of ethics out-perform in financial and other indicators those companies who say they do not have a code.

Companies are under growing pressure to disclose information – many have done this by producing separate reports:

- findings from a recent survey in the UK found that 132 of the FTSE 250 UK companies (and 90 of the FTSE 100) now report on some aspect of their sustainability performance; of these, 98 report on both social and environmental performance.

Few, however, have highlighted the issues that are the most relevant or have integrated SEE information with standard investor communications:

- SRI investors and wider opinion-formers have complained that corporate sustainability reports remain largely unread by mainstream investors, and that companies are failing to integrate the important messages in their standard annual report and accounts and their presentations to mainstream analysts

- less than one in five UK pension fund trustees believes that companies are providing sufficient information to enable interested parties to effectively assess environmental and social impacts and risks.

- the Association of British Insurers (ABI) has reported that by the end of 2003 only 23 of the FTSE 100 comprehensively disclosed their environmental and social risks – in line with the ABI's guidelines. A further 57 companies had moderate disclosure. Commitment is weaker still in the FTSE 250, with half of firms failing to achieve anything beyond moderate disclosure

- an Environmental Agency survey found that 89 per cent of FTSE AllShare companies discuss their interaction with the environment in their annual reports and accounts, but the majority lack depth, rigour or quantification; 11 per cent (63 companies) disclose nothing at all. Only 11 per cent of FTSE 350 companies link environmental issues to financial performance and just 5 per cent link environmental issues to shareholder value.

Appendix 1 Key facts

There is no transparent process for companies to identify which issues to report on. Investors ask about issues that differ from those on which companies report. Several points arise from this:

- careful analysis of sustainability reports leads to the conclusion that there is not yet an emerging "template" for property and construction companies. This makes the reading of each report a "journey of discovery", but it does not lend itself to ready comparability

- although several property and construction company sustainability reports identify their "most significant impacts", very few are explicit about the process they have employed to establish their significance

- an analysis of the tools and indices in use by SRI investors to differentiate between companies on the basis of their sustainability performance, found that the large majority are pan-industry rather than being sector-specific. Thus they seek information about the same range of issues across all industries rather than being specifically based on those sustainability issues found to be of most relevance to particular sub-sectors or companies. Unsurprisingly, therefore, large discrepancies exist between what investors are asking about and what companies in the property and construction industries sectors are reporting on:

  ○ there is a distinct lack of consistency – both between company reports within the same sub-sectors and across different investors' engagement criteria

  ○ generally speaking, the more specific the sustainability issues, the greater the disparity and there also appears to be greater disparity on the social and economic areas of sustainability than there is on the environment.

Appendix 2 Sources of further information

The following tables provide references to good practice standards and benchmarks, as well as a series of guidance. This list provides examples of some of the tools available but is not exhaustive.

A2.1 INDICATORS, BENCHMARKS AND STANDARDS

	Benchmark/standard	Description	Contact	Relevance
1	AA1000 by AccountAbility	The AA1000 Assurance Standard, launched in 2003 by AccountAbility, seeks to provide a single approach that deals effectively with the qualitative and quantitative data that is used to judge an organisation's "sustainability disclosure and performance".	www.accountability.org.uk/aa1000	All industry sectors
2	Corporate Responsibility Index by Business in the Community (BitC) and Index of Corporate Environmental Engagement by Business in the Environment (BiE)	These indices are pan-industry benchmarks of corporate responsibility and corporate environmental engagement. They provide indications of the relative quality of companies' approach to managing, measuring and reporting their sustainability performance.	www.bitc.org.uk/	All industry sectors
3	BREEAM – Building Research Establishment Environmental Assessment Methodology	A methodology used to measure the environmental performance of building design and management. It is based on best practice and can be used as a standard for achieving Good, Very Good, or Excellent ratings. BREEAM covers a range of building types including offices, homes and retail units.	www.products.bre.co.uk/breeam	All property and construction
4	CIRIA C563 *Sustainable construction: company indicators*	This report describes a range of indicators to measure the sustainability of design and construction companies, and to measure progress in delivering more sustainable construction projects.	www.ciriabooks.com	Construction
5	CEEQUAL – Civil Engineering Environmental Quality Assessment and Award Scheme	A credit-based assessment framework looking at the environmental quality of civil engineering projects – a civil engineering equivalent to BREEAM for buildings.	www.ceequal.com	Civil engineering and construction
6	Considerate Constructors Scheme	A voluntary code of practice, driven by the industry, that seeks to minimise any disturbance – including noise, dust and offensive behaviour – to the immediate neighbourhood. It is a national scheme, but some local authorities also operate similar schemes.	www.ccscheme.org.uk/	Construction
7	Constructing Excellence KPIs (key performance indicators)	Constructing Excellence publishes KPI wall charts for the sector include *Respect for people* and *Environment*. CE wall charts also cover sub-sectors, including *Construction consultants*, *M&E contractors* and *Construction products industry*. The charts can be used by companies to benchmark their performance.	www.constructingexcellence.org.uk/	Construction
8	Construction Skills Certification Scheme (CSCS)	The CSCS card shows that an employee is considered to be competent at his or her job, lists any relevant certificates held and also shows that the holder has undergone health and safety awareness training or testing. Various levels are available depending qualifications and experience.	http://www.cscs.uk.com/	Construction
9	ECON 019	Energy Consumption Guide 19 *Energy use in offices* (1998) provides benchmarks for good and typical practice for different office types and is a useful means of comparison for property investors with office portfolios.	www.actionenergy.org.uk	Property (offices), construction

Appendix 2 Sources of further information

	Benchmark/standard	Description	Contact	Relevance
10	Energy certification methodologies (as required for compliance with the EU Energy Performance of Buildings Directive)	The EU Energy Performance of Buildings Directive (EPBD) was published in January 2003. The far-reaching provisions include minimum energy performance requirements for all new buildings and energy certification of all buildings. The EPBD will be implemented in the UK through amended Part L requirements of the Building Regulations.	www.diag.org.uk/pdf/EPD_Final.pdf www.diag.org.uk/pdf/odpm_PartL_consultation2004.pdf	All property and construction
11	Environmental benchmarks for shopping centres	This annual benchmarking survey is undertaken by Upstream to calculate quantitative energy, water and waste benchmarks (typical and good practice) for similar categories of shopping centres.	www.upstreamstrategies.co.uk	Property (retail)
12	Forest Stewardship Council	FSC is an independent, non-profit, non-governmental organisation. It runs a global forest certification scheme which includes two key aspects: Forest Management and Chain of Custody certification to act as a guarantee that timber and wood products come from well-managed forests.	www.fsc-uk.info/	All industry sectors
13	Housing Quality Indicators	The HQI system is a measurement and assessment tool designed to allow all potential or existing housing schemes to be evaluated on the basis of quality. It encompasses indicators grouped under three main categories: Location, Design and Performance.	www.hqiuk.com/	House-builders
14	Insight WWF One Million Sustainable Homes	A survey of 13 of the UK's largest listed house-builders on all aspects of sustainability was published in January 2004 in a report entitled *Building towards sustainability*. Commissioned by WWF in conjunction with Insight Investment, it covers areas such as house-builders' impacts on the environment and society, and examines their governance, strategies and risk management.	www.wwf.org.uk/	House-builders
15	Investment Property Databank	IPD produces property market indices and portfolio benchmarks of financial performance for the property industry.	www.ipdindex.co.uk/	Commercial property
16	Investors in People	IiP is a national standard that sets out a level of good practice for employment policies, particularly in staff training and development to achieve business goals.	www.iipuk.co.uk/	All industry sectors
17	ISO 14001	ISO 14001 is the international standard for the certification of environmental management systems. Reviewed periodically by accredited auditors, it provides assurance that organisations are implementing procedures to minimise environmental risk and harm.	www.iso.org	All industry sectors
18	ISO 9001	ISO 9001 is an international standard for the certification of quality management system systems. It provides a framework to help ensure a common-sense approach which is reviewed periodically by accredited auditors.	www.iso.org	All industry sectors
19	Landfill Directive	The Landfill Directive 1999/31/EC is being implemented into UK legislation through The Landfill (England and Wales) Regulations 2002. The objective of the Directive is to prevent or reduce as far as possible negative effects on the environment from the landfilling of waste, by introducing stringent technical requirements for waste and landfills. It bans a wide variety of wastes from being landfilled including certain hazardous and other wastes (eg. contaminated soil).	http://europa.eu.int/comm/environment/waste/landfill_index.htm	All industry sectors

Appendix 2   Sources of further information

	Benchmark/standard	Description	Contact	Relevance
20	London Benchmarking Model	This model benchmarks companies against one another on the basis of their community "inputs" (eg investment both in cash and in kind), and "outputs" (eg the community and company benefits they achieve).	www.lbg-online.net/	All industry sectors
21	OHSAS 18001	The OHSAS is a recognised standard for the certification of occupational health and safety management systems. It enables an organisation to control relevant risks and improve its performance.	www.osha-bs8800-ohsas-18001-health-and-safety.com/ohsas-18001.htm	All industry sectors
22	SA 8000	A recognised standard for the workplace that covers all key labour rights including child labour, discrimination, and working hours.	www.cepaa.org/	All industry sectors
23	SAP ratings	The Standard Assessment Procedure Rating is included in Part L of the Building Regulations. SAP ratings relate to energy efficiency and are relevant to all new dwellings and those converted through material change of use.	www.natenergy.org.uk/enrate2.htm	House-builders
24	Secured by design	Secured by Design is an initiative led by the police aimed at designing-out crime by use of effective crime prevention and security standards that can be used for a range of development types.	www.securedbydesign.com/	All property and construction
25	Sustainable Code for Buildings	A voluntary code being developed in response to the recommendations of the Sustainable Buildings Task Group, which was set up by ODPM, DTI and DEFRA to establish higher standards for resource efficiency and CO_2 emissions. Scheduled for completion by 2006	www.dti.gov.uk/construction/sustain/sbtg.htm	All industry sectors
26	Sustainable Communities Plan	The Sustainable Communities Plan: Building for the Future was launched by the UK Government in February 2003 to create and maintain places in which people want to live and to address the serious housing shortages in London and the South East, as well as the impact of housing abandonment in the North and Midlands.	www.odpm.gov.uk/communities/index.htm www.odpm.gov.uk/communities/index.htm	House-builders, other property and construction

A2.2   GOOD PRACTICE GUIDANCE

	Benchmark/standard	Description	Contact	Relevance
27	Combined Code on Corporate Governance	The latest version of the Combined Code (2003) contains main and supporting principles and provisions and the existing Listing Rules require listed companies to make a disclosure statement in relation to the Code. The 2003 full version of the Code includes the Smith, Higgs and Turnbull guidance that came before it	www.fsa.gov.uk/pubs/ukla/lr_comcode2003.pdf	All industry sectors
28	Indicators that count: social and environmental indicators – a model for reporting impact	BiTC report that presents indicators to help companies decide what is most relevant and to report social and environmental impacts effectively.	www.bitc.org.uk/resources/publications/indicators.html	All industry sectors
29	The Natural Step	This is a sustainability management model that helps companies to integrate sustainability principles into their core strategies, decisions, operations and bottom line. It is founded on scientific principles based on natural limits of the earth's functional capacity.	www.naturalstep.org/	All industry sectors
30	SIGMA guidelines	SIGMA (Sustainability – Integrated Guidelines for Management) is a suite of guidelines aimed at embedding sustainability in an organisation through robust management practices.	www.projectsigma.com/	All industry sectors

Appendix 2 Sources of further information

	Benchmark/standard	Description	Contact	Relevance
31	Sustainability Works	Sustainability Works is a powerful online tool for anyone wanting guidance on the practicalities of achieving sustainable housing development and regeneration. It includes developing policies, setting targets, and assessment against benchmarks.	www.sustainabilityworks.org.uk	All property and construction
SUSTAINABILITY/CSR REPORTING AND COMMUNICATION				
32	ABI *Disclosure guidelines on socially responsible investment*	Guidelines on what investment institutions would expect to see included in the annual report of listed companies. Specifically they refer to disclosures relating to board responsibilities and to policies, procedures and verification. SRI investors cite compliance with these guidelines as the minimum standard for inclusions in annual reports.	www.abi.org.uk/Display/File/85/SRI_Guidelines.doc	All industry sectors
33	GRI *Sustainability reporting guidelines 2002*	The Global Reporting Initiative is an international initiative to develop globally applicable sustainability reporting guidelines. Organisations can use the guidelines when reporting the economic, environmental and social dimensions of their activities. It is widely considered to represent best practice in the production of standalone sustainability reports.	www.globalreporting.org	All industry sectors
34	*General guidelines on environmental reporting* (November 2001)	These guidelines were issued by UK Government to help explain how to produce an environmental report, outline its main contents and suggest key indicators to report against. They also include a possible incremental approach to help organisations plan staged improvements in their reporting. Although the guidelines are aimed particularly at organisations new to reporting, experienced reporters might also find them useful. Specific guidelines have also been produced for reporting on: • water (December 2000) • waste (June 2000) • greenhouse gas emissions (revised December 2003)	www.defra.gov.uk/environment/envrp/general/index.htm	All industry sectors
35	The GHG Indicator: UNEP Guidelines for Calculating Greenhouse Gas Emissions for Businesses and Non-Commercial Organisations	These Guidelines were issued by the United Nations Environment Programme (UNEP) and provide a step-by-step method for calculating the emissions of greenhouse gases (GHGs). They show how these can be combined to give a single GHG 'Indicator' which is applicable to companies regardless of their size.	www.uneptie.org/energy/publications/files/ghgind.htm	All industry sectors
36	*OFR – practical guidance for directors* (May 2004)	Draft Regulations requiring all UK quoted companies to produce operating and financial reviews (OFRs) were published in May 2004. This practical guidance covers the need to include details of a company's objectives and strategies, and to provide information on "a wide range of factors which may be relevant to an understanding of the business, such as information about employees, environmental matters and community and social issues".	www.dti.gov.uk/cld/pdfs/ofr_guide.pdf	All industry sectors
37	*Sustainable development reporting – striking the balance* (December 2002)	This report was published by the World Business Council on Sustainable Development. It presents a step-by-step set of questions and answers designed to prompt companies to think through the process of reporting.	www.wbcsd.org	All industry sectors

Appendix 2 Sources of further information

A2.3 USEFUL ORGANISATIONS

	Name of organisation	Brief description	Website details
38	Association of Chartered Certified Accountants	ACCA co-ordinates annual high-profile awards for sustainability, social and environmental reporting.	www.accaglobal.com/social_environmental/
39	CSR Academy	The Academy aims to promote CSR learning through the first dedicated CSR Competency Framework. It is for companies of all sizes as well as for UK educational institutions.	www.csracademy.org.uk/about.htm
40	Department for the Environment, Food and Rural Affairs (Defra)	UK central government department with responsibility for environment policy, among other areas.	www.defra.gov.uk
41	Department of Trade and Industry (DTI)	UK central government department with responsibility for trade policy, among other areas. The DTI has created a specialised gateway for information on CSR which covers all government-related CSR initiatives.	www.dti.gov.uk www.csr.gov.uk
42	Dow Jones Sustainability Indices	Launched in 1999, the Dow Jones Sustainability Indexes are the first global indexes tracking the financial performance of the leading sustainability-driven companies worldwide. Based on the co-operation of Dow Jones Indexes, STOXX Limited and SAM they provide asset managers with objective benchmarks to manage sustainability portfolios.	www.sustainability-indexes.com/
43	Ethical Investment Research Service (EIRIS)	EIRIS Services Ltd, a subsidiary company of EIRIS (a charity set up in 1983 to look at the social, environmental and ethical performance of companies), provides an ethical investment research service to business clients such as fund managers and financial institutions, and a service for private investors.	www.eiris.org/
44	FTSE/FTSE4Good	The FTSE4Good Index Series is designed to measure the performance of companies that meet globally recognised corporate responsibility standards, and to facilitate investment in those companies. FTSE4Good indices are often used by financial companies to inform their creation of socially responsible investment products.	www.ftse.com/ftse4good
45	London Stock Exchange	The LSE runs the UK equity markets and trading services, and co-ordinates the Corporate Responsibility Exchange, a service launched in 2004 in which companies disclose their CSR information, which is then made available to subscribing institutional investors.	www.londonstockexchange.com/
46	PIRC	Pensions & Investment Research Consultants Ltd (PIRC) is the UK's principal pension fund research house and its research is widely used by pension funds pursuing practical and effective SRI policies.	www.pirc.co.uk/
47	SAM Research Inc	SAM Group is responsible for tracking the financial performance of leading sustainability-driven companies worldwide and co-ordinating the analysis for the Dow Jones Sustainability Index (DJSI). These indices select leading companies for investment purposes on the basis of the quality of the company's strategy and management and its performance in dealing with opportunities and risks deriving from economic, environmental and social developments.	www.sam-group.com/htmle/main.cfm www.sustainability-indexes.com
48	UKSIF	The UK Social Investment Forum is the membership network for SRI investors. It may provide a useful reference for those investors wishing to develop their SRI policy, and provides useful information for investors	www.uksif.org